THOMAS ALVA EDISON
INVENTOR

THOMAS ALVA
EDISON
INVENTOR

RUTH CROMER WEIR

Illustrated by Albert Orbaan

ABINGDON PRESS
New York • *Nashville*

To my husband

KENNETH J. WEIR

THOMAS ALVA EDISON'S own accounts, told with the thoroughness of a great scientist, have furnished the background for most of the action and the exciting inventions in this book. Acknowledgment is also due to the Thomas Alva Edison Foundation in Orange, New Jersey; John Coakley, chairman of the Edison Birthday Committee; Maud Lamley, librarian of Milan, Ohio; to my husband, for his technical engineering advice; and to Edison's many friends and neighbors and their descendants for their valuable help and information.

RUTH CROMER WEIR

CONTENTS

CHAPTER ONE

• THE SILVER COIN •

"Now will you go to bed, Alvie?" Tannie Edison begged. "You know I promised Mother and Father to put you to bed after they went out."

Thomas Alva Edison, two years old, was scrubbed clean. He had on his long nightgown, ready for bed. But he did not want to go. He burrowed deeper into the rocking chair beside his big sister. The chair squeaked comfortably. It was the only sound in the little red brick house.

Slyly Tom looked up into Tannie's face. "I like Sam, too," he said.

"How did you know Sam was coming?"

Tannie demanded, her cheeks pink.

Tom did not have to answer. There was a knock at the door. He rushed to open it.

"Hello, Tannie. Hello, Alvie." Sam Bailey's collar looked high and stiff, his hair slick. Tom thought he was the handsomest young man in Milan, Ohio.

"You still up?" Sam asked, patting Tom's blond head.

"He won't go to bed." Hopelessly Tannie sank down on the sofa. Sam sat beside her.

Tom climbed up and wedged his little body in between them. The sofa was covered with stiff cloth made from horsehair. It pricked through his thin nightgown. He squirmed uncomfortably, but still refused to go to bed.

At last Sam grinned and reached in his pocket.

Suddenly a bright, silver object was rolling across the floor. It spun around and around before it stopped.

Tom squealed with delight. He jumped down and ran to pick it up. He looked at one side. He turned it over and studied the other side.

"Read. Read," Tom cried. He took the coin to Tannie.

"1847!" Tannie read. "Why, that's the year you were born, Alvie."

"He may have it—if he'll go to bed," Sam offered.

"Oh, Sam! You shouldn't!"

From the look of surprise on Tannie's face, Tom knew that the shiny thing must be valuable. He rubbed his tiny fingers over the grooves cut around the edge. He felt the smooth, polished surface. It was so round, so perfect! Even to feel it was exciting for a time. Then he gave it back to Sam.

"Make it go! Make it go!" he shouted.

Once more Sam spun the silver piece.

Flat on his stomach, in the middle of the

floor, Tom watched. Rolling, rolling it came toward him like a magic wheel. What held it up? What made it go?

Tom cried out in delight and wonder.

At last, satisfied with the idea of having the wonderful coin for his own, Tom agreed to go to bed. Tannie laughed happily and hugged him tightly as she tucked him in.

Tom reached under the pillow to feel his silver coin. He did not know its value. He knew only that it was round, and bright, and perfect. And that it could go faster than anything he had ever seen.

"In the morning I will spin it," he whispered as he fell asleep. "And it will go—and go."

CHAPTER TWO

· FIRST EXPERIMENT ·

"Shoo! Go away, you stubborn hen!" Six-year-old Tom waved his arms.

He had slipped away from home. Half running, half sliding, he had rushed down the bank behind the house. A canal ran along the foot of the bank. Tom thought the canal much more exciting than the quiet little street where he lived.

He had found the hen in a barn behind a warehouse along the canal. She was sitting on a nest of eggs. She gave him a glassy stare.

"Move over!" Tom commanded. He had a plan he wanted to try. "I'll help you."

Naw! Naw! Naw! Naw! The hen objected harshly. Her feathers bristled.

"Yes!" Tom tried to push her from the nest.

Cut caaaaah! she screamed. Suddenly she was all beak and claws and beating wings.

Tom fled. From a few feet away, he watched her cautiously.

Just then a bell rang. A ship was coming up the canal.

"Whoa there!" Now the mules that towed the ship through the canal were stopping.

Tom listened for the rumble of wagons and more wagons. They brought wheat from the fields in the country to the warehouses on the canal. There the wagons dumped their loads into great bins. Ships came to get the golden grain and carry it up the canal to the Great Lakes.

Again Tom heard the exciting sound of the ship's bell.

He hesitated a moment. He wanted to see the ship and watch the men load it. But he turned back to the hen. His mind was made up. He had heard that hens hatched eggs by sitting on them. He had decided to try hatching eggs himself. Nothing would stop him.

Once more Tom tried to push the hen from her nest. Once more she pecked and scratched at the blond hair and chubby hands. But she was no match for the determined boy. Screeching, she flew from the barn.

Eagerly Tom climbed into the nest and sat down. There was a strange cracking sound. "Is this the way eggs hatch?" he asked in wonder.

All afternoon Tom stayed on the nest. The broken eggs oozed through his clothes, making him uncomfortable. Long shadows began to creep close. The sky grew red from the setting sun. But Tom did not leave. At last he heard a voice.

"Alvie! Alvie! Where are you?" It was his big sister, coming to look for him.

Tom did not answer. Tannie would only take him home. The eggs might be hatching any time now, he reasoned. He did not want to leave.

A few minutes later his father found him. Mr. Edison was a cheerful man, tall and handsome. "Whatever are you doing?" he asked.

"Hatching eggs," answered Tom.

"W-H-A-T?"

"The hen sits on eggs. So can I."

Hopelessly Tom's father saw the mess of eggs and straw on his son. For a moment he looked into Tom's serious gray eyes. Then he called Tannie.

"Take him home," he said. He seemed glad to go back to his shingle factory and leave Tom in his sister's care.

"Oh! Just look at you! What will Mother say?" Tannie grabbed Tom's sticky hand.

They climbed the steep hill to the house. Tannie seemed to go faster and faster. It was hard for Tom to keep up with her.

Earlier that afternoon he had slipped down that same hill so fast, he remembered. "Why is a hill bigger going *up?*" he asked Tannie.

Almost always Tannie answered his questions. But now they crossed the back yard in silence.

"Mother," cried Tannie as they reached the door. "I think Alvie needs a good, sound spanking. He broke a whole nest of eggs. And how do you suppose he did it? *Sitting* on them!"

Tom's mother looked up in surprise. She closed the oven door by the wide fireplace. "I thought you were watching him, Tannie," she said gently. "Hurry and put some water on to heat before your father comes."

Mrs. Edison leaned over to help her young son.

Tom looked searchingly into the face so much like his own. "Mother," he asked, "tell me, please. Why didn't the eggs hatch?"

"A good question deserves a good answer, son," Mrs. Edison said. "Eggs must be kept warm for several weeks before they hatch."

Tom nodded. "They were warm," he said.

"The hen is very careful not to break the delicate eggs," Mrs. Edison went on. "Now

• 18 •

you must get cleaned up," she said firmly.

Mrs. Edison rubbed a soapy cloth over Tom's face. She had been a teacher before she married Samuel Edison, and she believed in doing a thorough job.

Tom squirmed as she scrubbed.

"Careful. Don't get soap in your eyes," she warned.

He sputtered, blowing bubbles. But the word he was trying to say could not be mistaken.

"How—How—"

Across the room Tannie gave a little groan.

Tom looked into his mother's sweet, patient face. Gratefully he saw that she was listening for his next question.

CHAPTER THREE

· QUESTIONS AND ANSWERS ·

Tom watched his mother turn up the wick of the lamp. She scratched a match and held the flame against the wick. It sputtered as though gasping for breath.

"Why does it cough like that?" asked Tom.

"Perhaps the wick is not soaked well enough with oil," his mother answered.

Tom looked in the glass bowl of the lamp. "There is plenty of oil," he said.

Mrs. Edison carefully fitted the chimney in place. The flame licked the glass, leaving a black spot of carbon. The lamp flickered, and the carbon made a shadow that danced on the wall.

Tom's eyes gleamed with interest. "It's a kitten," he cried, running to the wall. In delight he pointed to the arched back and fluffy tail of the shadow. "How does the lamp make pictures like that?" he asked.

"Perhaps William will make you some pictures. Then you can hold them before the lamp and watch their shadows," Mrs. Edison suggested.

After supper Tom leaned over his big brother's drawing board. Tom loved to watch William draw.

"Make a ship. And a rabbit. And a house. And a chicken." Tom waited with scissors to cut out the pictures.

He watched the shadow delightedly as he held each picture in front of the lamp and jiggled it up and down. "Look at it move!" he cried.

It was hard for William to draw with shadows dancing over his paper. At last he complained good-naturedly. "Hey! Get that chicken off my railroad track."

"Railroad?" With a bound, Tom was back at his brother's elbow.

There was no railroad in Milan. But Tom had heard much talk of trains and railroads. Some people in Milan did not want a railroad to come through their town. They were afraid it would take away the shipping business on the canal. Tom's father wanted a railroad. He believed it would be good for business.

Tom wanted a railroad, too, but for different reasons. "Oh, what fun it would be to have engines chugging through town!" he exclaimed. "Bells ringing. Whistles blowing. And big wheels rolling, rolling."

He looked at the picture on William's drawing board. He studied the engine, the tender, the baggage car, the passenger car, and the freight cars behind. Then, suddenly, he asked a question.

"Why did you make the track bigger in the front than in the back?"

The question seemed to echo in the little room. Tom's father laid down his newspaper. His mother held her darning needle still.

William looked at his little brother. He had asked a question which was hard to answer. But Tom's next question helped to explain.

"The track isn't *really* smaller in the back, is it?"

"No."

"Then why do you make it that way?"

"Things look smaller the farther away you are from them," William said slowly. "If there was a big elephant far away, I would draw it smaller than a little mouse close up."

Tom's eyes were round.

William added a little teasingly, "The relationship between size and distance in a picture is called *perspective*."

Tom was not to be stopped by a big word.

His response was prompt. "Why?"

"Oh, I don't know," answered William.

"Why don't you know?"

Tom's mother rose from her chair. "Now it is bedtime," she said firmly.

She took a candle from the shelf and held it high to light the dark stairway. "Another day will soon be here," she promised.

Each new day brought new questions for Tom. Why is a ship's keel so deep in the water? What happens to wheat in a bin? How fast can fire burn?

Tom had many exciting and dangerous adventures in finding out the answers.

At dinner one day Mr. Edison kept looking at his son. Finally he spoke. "Lockwood tells me they'll have to hire an extra man at his shipyard."

"Oh, is business better?" Mrs. Edison inquired with interest.

"No." Tom's father shook his head.

"Then why does the shipyard need more help?"

Tom squirmed uneasily as his father looked at him again.

"The way Lockwood puts it, they need a man to answer our son's questions. What were you doing at Lockwood's?" Mr. Edison asked Tom.

"I was finding out how to build a ship. Now I know why the keel must be deep in the water. It helps keep the ship from tipping over."

Tom was eager to tell what he had learned. The family listened in amazement.

"You should not bother the men at work," Mr. Edison cautioned Tom.

For several days Tom remembered. Down at the canal he watched farmers unload wheat in the great bins. Then he watched the wheat loaded into ships.

He wondered what happened inside the bins. So he climbed in the top of one. A farmer

was emptying his wagon. From a rafter Tom watched the grain whirl beneath him. He leaned farther to see better. His hand slipped. Suddenly he was in the wheat. It began to cover him like a great smothering blanket.

Tom tried to get his breath, and choked. Wheat filled his throat and nose. He fought to get out. But he only buried himself deeper.

Then, faintly, he heard men shouting, "Quick! A boy fell in!"

Tom never knew how they saved him. He found himself in the center of a group of men with shovels and ropes.

"He's coming around," said one. "Thank God, we were in time!"

Then Tom saw his father. His face looked white and his voice shook as he said, "You'd better go home to Mother."

For a while Tom could feel the smothering wheat over him whenever he passed the warehouses. He did not play along the canal. Instead, he went to the Huron River at the edge of town. There, in the hot summer months, he learned to swim and to skip stones over the water.

Fall came. The leaves on the maple trees turned bright red and yellow, and fell to the ground. Tom helped his father rake them into smoky bonfires.

One day Tom tried to light a fire by himself. A wind whisked through the yard and swept the leaves away. Tom collected more leaves. This time he took them to a neighbor's barn. There, he reasoned, the wind could not blow the leaves away.

He lit a match, and the leaves caught quickly.

Pouf! A pile of straw nearby went up in flames. Suddenly the whole inside of the barn was burning.

"Fire!" Tom cried as he ran outside.

Men, women, and children came running to help put out the fire. The flames leaped higher and higher. Then they died away, leaving only a pile of ashes.

"How did the fire start?" someone asked.

"Yes. How did it start?" cried the others.

For a moment Tom hesitated, his face red. How could he explain? Then he spoke up.

"I did it. I just started a little bonfire. I didn't mean to burn the barn."

The people shook their heads. But no one

there doubted that Tom was telling the truth.

"Come home with me," said Mrs. Edison. She put her arm around her son's shoulders. "Your father will talk to the owner."

When they reached home, Tom looked uneasily toward the big clock which stood in the corner. Behind the clock Mrs. Edison kept a switch. She did not hesitate to use it when she thought Tom needed discipline.

Tom was relieved when his mother sat down and picked up her sewing.

"I am glad you spoke up, son," she said. "What's done is done. Never cry over spilt milk."

When Tom's father came home he took Tom with him to see the neighbor whose barn had burned. Mr. Edison offered to pay for the barn.

"No. That old barn should have been torn down years ago," the owner said. He looked at Tom's earnest face. "I'm convinced your boy meant no harm but we've got to show the boys they can't burn down barns. Your son must be punished."

Tom waited anxiously for the man to speak.

"I propose to whip your son. In public!"

Tom's father hesitated. Then slowly he nodded his head.

The trip to the town square was only a few blocks. It seemed miles to Tom as he followed the neighbor. A noisy group of boys collected. Tom hung his head in shame.

Afterward he walked home without speaking to anyone. He started to open the front gate.

"Hey, Tom!" the older boy who lived across the street called. "How was it?"

"Well," Tom spoke thoughtfully. "The licking wasn't half as bad as the going to get it."

CHAPTER FOUR

• PORT HURON TOWER •

Trains on the new railroad south of Milan traveled faster than ships on the canal. More and more farmers took their wheat to the railroad. There was less and less business in Milan. And Tom's father sold fewer shingles.

When Tom was seven years old the Edisons moved to Port Huron, Michigan. This was a busy town about fifty miles northeast of Detroit. Mr. Edison went into the grain, feed, and lumber business.

Tom wandered through the big rooms of the new home. He felt lost.

"Why don't you go out and play?" suggested his sister. Tannie and Mrs. Edison were hanging crisp ruffled curtains at the windows of the large house.

Outside, Tom looked at the land his father had bought with the house which faced Fort Gratiot. A big grove of trees gave the new home its name—"House in the Grove."

Tom saw little to interest him. "Ten acres of land!" he said. "It might as well be a big ocean." He wandered over to the St. Clair River nearby.

He wished the next house, half a mile away, were closer. He wished for other houses, and barns, and busy warehouses. He longed to be back in his old home in Milan.

Suddenly Tom saw a team of horses and a wagon coming up the road. He ran to the house.

"Whoa there!" A big boy in his early teens jumped off the wagon.

"This is Michael Oates," explained Tom's father. "He's going to help with the chores.

And he's going to teach you how to farm."

For a moment the boys looked at each other.

The bigger boy grinned good-naturedly. "Just call me Mike," he said.

"Call me Al," Tom replied happily.

That afternoon he helped Mike unload the wagon. There was a shiny new plow. There were rakes and spades and hoes. And in the bottom of the wagon Tom found hammers and saws and some heavy lumber.

"What is that for?" he asked.

"Beats me," said Mike, scratching his head.

That evening at supper Mr. Edison explained that he was planning to build a high tower. "We'll let visitors climb the tower and look through a telescope. They will be able to see over the country for miles and miles. I'm going to make the tower a hundred feet high."

"A hundred feet!" Tom exclaimed. "That'll

be the highest tower in America, won't it? When do we start building?"

"Hold your horses, son!" Mr. Edison smiled. "When the garden is planted, we will start work on the tower."

And so a new and busy life began for Tom. For several summers he helped in the garden. He learned how to plow the soil, plant seeds, and cultivate the crops.

The crops grew, and the tower also grew. One day Tom and Mike loaded vegetables into a cart Mr. Edison had bought. They hitched the horse, Old Nell, to the cart and set off on their first selling adventure.

"Best vegetables in the whole world! Radishes! Onions! Carrots!" Tom cried out through the streets of Port Huron.

"Boys! Boys!" the housewives called.

Tom and Mike did a big business.

On the way home Tom jingled the money in his pocket. He did not mind selling the vegetables. It was raising them that was hard work.

"Building a tower is lots more fun," he said. He urged Old Nell to go faster. The cart rattled along the road. Soon they were near home.

"The platform is up!" cried Tom excitedly. "See how much taller it is than our house!"

That evening Mr. Edison said, "Tomorrow we can begin making the circular stairway."

"What is that?" asked Tom.

"A stairway that goes around and around."

"Why will you make it that way?" Tom asked.

Then suddenly his eyes brightened. "I see," he said. He grabbed a pencil. "For every step *up* you have to have as much space *out*. Why, a regular stairway would go clear across our yard." He laughed. "Wouldn't that look funny?"

"Yes," agreed Mr. Edison, surprised both

that Tom understood so quickly and that he could draw so well.

Men in Port Huron came to help finish the stairway. Mr. Edison put up a telescope on the platform. The tower was ready for business. Mr. Edison charged visitors twenty-five cents to climb the stairs and look through the telescope.

"How would you like to be gatekeeper and collect the money?" Tom's father asked.

Tom thought that would be an interesting job. But Sunday after Sunday passed. Few visitors came. In two months Tom collected only three dollars.

Then one Sunday the railroad ran a special train to Port Huron so people could visit Mr. Edison's tower. Six hundred people climbed the steps and exclaimed over the view.

That was an exciting day for Tom. After the visitors left, he helped his father count the money.

ENTRANCE
← EDISON TOWER
TELESCOPE

GEN'L
ADMISS
25¢

"A hundred and fifty dollars. That will just about pay for the tower," Mr. Edison said.

He stroked his beard thoughtfully. "You tell me you don't like gardening."

"No, Father, I don't. It's hard work."

"How much did you and Mike make this summer on your vegetables?"

Tom did not know. He was not very interested. He had always given the money to his mother as soon as he reached home.

"Mother says you made six hundred dollars."

"Six hundred dollars!" Tom was surprised that the garden had made so much. The tower was fun, but it had not made much money.

"Well," Tom reasoned, "I guess hard work pays."

CHAPTER FIVE

• THE "ADDLED" SCHOOLBOY •

Tom was worried.

He stuffed a big cookie in his mouth and washed it down with milk. Then he asked the question that worried him.

"Mother, what does 'addled' mean?"

Mrs. Edison was rolling out cookies on the table.

"Addled means mixed up—confused," she explained. "Sometimes we say a person is addled if he does not know what he is doing. Why do you ask?"

"The teacher told the inspector I was addled," Tom blurted out unhappily.

"Why, son! Are you sure you did not make

a mistake?" Mrs. Edison asked.

"I'm sure. I have to sit in the front seat."

Mrs. Edison slipped off her apron. "We're going back to school before the teacher gets away. Run and tell Mike to hitch up quickly."

The teacher was still at school when Tom and Mrs. Edison arrived. He invited Mrs. Edison to sit down.

Tom's mother wasted no time. "Did you tell the inspector my son was *addled?*" she asked.

The teacher hesitated. Tom wondered what he would say.

"Yes, I did," he finally answered. "Though I did not know Tom was listening. I might as well tell you, Mrs. Edison. Your son has learned nothing in three months of school. In my opinion he never will learn anything."

Tom felt his mother's hand tighten on his. Her cheeks had turned bright pink.

"I am glad I understand how you feel," she said. "I knew my son was learning little in school. But I hoped you would find the time and patience to teach an especially bright boy. I was wrong to expect it. Good day, sir."

The teacher's mouth dropped open, but Mrs. Edison gave him no chance to reply. She turned and left the school, her skirts swishing.

His mother believed in him! Hot tears of gratitude filled Tom's eyes. The unhappiness of the weeks he had spent in school seemed to slip away.

They were almost home when his mother spoke. "How would you like to have me teach you?"

"I wouldn't have to go to school?" Tom could hardly believe it was true. His mother would not scold him when he asked questions. His eyes shone. Then doubts came to his mind.

"But you taught in high school! Could you teach first grade?"

"It will not take you long to learn to read and write," said Mrs. Edison. Then you can study—and learn—just as fast as you wish. Stories. Geography. History. Science books. Writing. Numbers."

His mother made lessons sound interesting.

"When can we start? Tomorrow?" Tom asked excitedly.

Mrs. Edison nodded.

"Mother, I will study hard. I will do anything you tell me." Gratefully he threw his arms around her and hugged her tightly.

Tom kept his promise. With his mother's help, he soon learned to read. "Now I will read every book we have," he said, looking at the bookshelves. "I'll start on the top shelf."

Mr. Edison looked up from his newspaper. "I will pay you twenty-five cents for every book you read," he promised.

"Storybooks, too?"

"Well—"

"His education would be one-sided if he had no stories," Tom's mother spoke up. "A boy with imagination needs them."

"Yes, I suppose so," Mr. Edison agreed. "But you must report on every book."

After that, Tom read several books every week and collected his money. He learned to write beautifully. But he did not care for mathematics. He studied every day. The rest of the time he read, or helped Mike.

One day he asked his friend, "How would you like to go up in the air like a balloon?"

"Why, I couldn't do that!" Mike laughed.

"Yes, you could," promised Tom. "We'll fill you with gas!"

"How?"

"You know how your stomach swells up with gas when you take Seidlitz powders?"

"Seidlitz powders! Go away!"

"I didn't mean *one* dose," said Tom. "I meant three. Three doses should fill you so full you'd be lighter than air!"

Mike could think of no argument.

"One, two, three," Tom whipped a spoon from his pocket. Quickly he measured out the powder and gave it to Mike.

"Is your stomach swelling up?"

"Yes!"

"How do you feel? Are you getting light?"

"I feel terrible!" groaned Mike. His face turned pale green. He became very sick.

Suddenly Tom was frightened. He ran to get his mother.

Mrs. Edison put Mike to bed. She made sure that he was all right. Then she brought the switch from behind the clock.

Tom knew that he deserved the whipping. But his experiments had not ended. A few days later he found a book which told how to perform simple experiments in physics.

"Mother," cried Tom excitedly, "this is the most wonderful book I have ever seen! I'm going to try every experiment myself!"

Mrs. Edison let Tom make a laboratory in

the basement. He built shelves for equipment. With Mike's help he collected two hundred bottles. He carefully marked each bottle POISON.

"What are you going to put in all those bottles?" asked Mike.

Already Tom was busy filling them. "Sulphur. Beeswax. Vinegar. Feathers. Mercury. Wool. Cotton. Some hair—"

He looked at Mike's unruly hair. Then he remembered his experience with gas. He reached up and snipped off a lock from his own head.

"Real experiments! In a real laboratory!" Tom's eyes were shining. His great lifework was beginning.

During the next months Tom performed many experiments. He kept a notebook and wrote down every experiment. He drew pictures to help explain his work.

He turned a glass upside down on a pan of water. The air inside the glass kept it from sinking. He ran across a piece of carpet, then touched paper dolls. They danced with the electric shock. He set up a little machine with a magnet which could produce electricity.

Strange smells and sounds began to come from the basement. "The whole house smells like rotten eggs," Mrs. Edison complained. "I'm afraid you may even blow up the place.

You must clear out that mess from the cellar at once!"

"Just when I have a good start in chemistry," Tom wailed. "That smell is *good*. It shows I did the experiment right."

Mrs. Edison finally said that Tom could keep his laboratory. But he must never bring any dangerous chemicals home. And he must keep the door closed.

But Tom had spent all his money. The wages he earned for reading would not go far. How could he buy the things he needed?

"I need a battery and chemicals," he said, deep in thought. Suddenly he had an idea. He ran up the basement steps and rushed from the house.

"Where are you going?" called Mrs. Edison.

Tom was running fast. He stopped only long enough to answer, "To look for a job!"

CHAPTER SIX

WORKING ON THE RAILROAD

Tom had his first chance at a real job when he was twelve years old. In 1859, the Grand Trunk Railroad began regular train service between Port Huron and Detroit. Every morning at seven o'clock the train left Port Huron. Every night it returned at nine-thirty.

Pung! Pung! The steam engine panted.

Standing on the station platform Tom examined every part of the engine. The giant wheels. The big cowcatcher in front. The smokestack on top.

Just then the fireman opened the firebox inside. Flames shot from the stack. Then, as the fireman put on wood, black smoke rolled out.

Again the engine panted *Pung! Pung!*

"Power!" Tom said. He tingled at the very thought of the power in the throbbing engine. Now the power was held in check. Soon the engineer would pull a lever called the throttle. The steam would furnish power to turn the great wheels. The train would move. How Tom wished he could be the one to pull the throttle!

"Be on the lookout for a good trainboy," the conductor told the station agent.

Tom whirled around to face the conductor.

"I could do it, sir."

The conductor looked down at Tom, who was small for his age. He began to chuckle, then stopped. The face he saw was eager and intelligent.

"Why, I believe you could," he said. "But first you must get your parents' consent."

Getting his parents' consent was not easy, but Tom was ready with arguments. Many boys of his age worked, he pointed out. He promised to bring his father newspapers and magazines.

Tom's mother feared the work would be too hard. She thought seven-thirty in the morning to nine-thirty at night was too long a day for a twelve-year-old boy.

"I can get dinner in Detroit," Tom said. "I can eat breakfast and supper at home."

Mrs. Edison finally agreed to let Tom work.

"I can see your heart is set on it," she said.

And so Tom began a new and exciting life as a trainboy. His job was to go through the train and sell newspapers and food to the passengers. He bought magazines and candy at low prices and sold them at a profit.

Tom kept his supplies in the baggage car.

"Candy! Peanuts! Juicy apples!" he shouted. He carried the food on a big tray.

"Papers! Magazines!" he cried on his next trip through the train.

Soon he learned the best ways to sell. If he made the trip every half hour the people were restless and they bought eagerly.

Business was good. Some days Tom made as much as ten dollars. Every day he paid his mother one dollar from the money he earned.

On his first day in Detroit Tom discovered the public library. He walked past shelf after shelf, marveling at the books.

"I will read every book here," he said.

Soon Tom gave up that idea. He had found the science books. He was anxious to try the experiments he read about.

One day he had an idea. Between his trips through the train he had time to spare. There was extra space in the baggage car. Why not ask the conductor if he could have a small laboratory on the train?

The next day Tom explained his plan to the

conductor. "I could have a rack for bottles. I wouldn't make any mess."

"Can't see any harm in it," the conductor said. "Just don't neglect your work."

Tom spent all his money on the new laboratory. Still, he did not have enough to buy all he wanted. Chemicals were expensive. He never had enough of them.

"How can I make more money?" Tom asked. He decided to expand his business. He hired a boy to sell candy and papers for him on a fast train to Detroit. He opened a fruit-and-vegetable shop in Port Huron and hired another boy. He also opened a newsstand.

One evening Tom came loaded with supplies to the train. He had candy, papers, magazines, fruits, and vegetables.

"Here comes the busiest boy in Michigan," the engineer called from his window.

"I'm never too busy to ride with you," laughed Tom.

"Put your baggage in. Make your run through the train. Then climb in here with me at the first stop," said the engineer. "I'll let you try your hand at the throttle."

Tom could hardly believe his luck. He had always wanted to run the engine. At the first stop he climbed into the engine cab.

The engineer pulled the throttle. The train started. Then the engineer gave Tom his seat.

The engineer and fireman had danced all night. Soon both men fell asleep.

"Now the train is mine," said Tom, feeling very big. He rang the bell. He blew the whistle. *Tooooot. Tooooot. Too-too!* It was the crossing whistle he knew so well.

The air became hot in the engine cab. Tom thought the boiler needed water. So he stopped for water at the next tank. Then he speeded up to twelve miles an hour.

Suddenly hot mud blew from the stack. It

covered everything. Mud on the engine. Mud in the cab. Mud on his face. Tom wondered if he should wake the engineer. Then the mud quit falling.

Tom slowed down to make a stop. There the fireman always poured oil in a cup on the front of the engine. Tom had seen the cup filled many times. But he did not know that the engineer turned off the steam first.

Confidently he climbed down from the cab and up on the cowcatcher, the way the fireman did. He opened the cup.

Steam hissed out. It almost knocked Tom off the engine. He pushed on the cup with all his strength. At last he managed to close it.

Back in the cab he decided to go without oil.

How thrilling it was to reach up and pull the throttle, then feel the engine go! He pulled the throttle farther toward him. The engine picked up speed.

Suddenly mud began to pour out again.

Ahead was the junction where the train always stopped. Tom pushed the throttle, and the train pulled up like a spouting volcano.

The trainmen woke up with a start.

"What is the matter?" Tom asked.

"She's got too much water in the boiler," the engineer laughed. "The water gets into the stack, and all the dirt and soot come spouting out."

Tom laughed with the men. Then he grew serious. He had felt so big at the throttle. He had thought he knew how to fill the oil cup. But he had failed to see that the steam must be turned off. He had never dreamed that a boiler could have too much water.

"I must pay better attention," he said. "I must be more careful. Each thing that is done may change the way a machine works."

Suddenly he knew that he had much to learn.

CHAPTER SEVEN

• UNUSUAL BUSINESS •

"Time and money. Those are the things I need most."

Tom brushed ink over his tiny printing press. He had bought it cheaply, hoping to make money with a little newspaper of his own. He was trying to earn enough money for batteries.

He had spent hours writing the news and setting the type. Now he must print each paper separately on the little press.

The train gave a sudden jerk. Ink spilled on the type. Tom did not want to waste it. He decided to print a test sheet of paper.

Carefully he laid the paper on the type. He

forced down the wood top of the press. Then he lifted it and peeled off the paper.

Tom grinned. What he saw first pleased him.

THE WEEKLY HERALD

PUBLISHED BY A. EDISON

TERMS

THE WEEKLY Eight Cents Per Month

Soon his look turned to one of dismay.

"The ads! Why did the ink have to spill on the ads?" he said. They were the most important part of his paper. He used them to advertise the butter and eggs he sold to the trainmen.

Tom was thinking as he wiped up the ink. He liked to write the paper. But the printing was tiresome work.

How long will it take to make enough money to buy batteries? he wondered. He was desperate for batteries to try out his new telegraph line.

Tom's friend, Jim Clancy, was also interested in the telegraph. Jim lived half a mile from Tom's house. Together they had strung a wire between their homes. The wire was only stovepipe wire. Bottles and rags were the insulation. Trees and fence posts served as telegraph poles.

The boys had learned the Morse Code— the dots and dashes and spaces used to send messages. Now the only thing they needed was batteries.

"Trainboy!" The conductor yelled in the baggage-car door, interrupting Tom's thoughts. "The passengers are asking for papers."

Tom grabbed his evening papers and started through the train. "Papers! Papers!" he cried.

"Nicodemus, pay the boy."

Tom looked curiously at two well-dressed gentlemen and their Negro servant. One of the men reached out. He took the papers and threw them out the window.

Tom's eyes bulged.

"Nicodemus, pay the boy,"

Nicodemus grinned. He reached in a bag and paid Tom.

Tom rushed back to the baggage car and returned with magazines.

One of the Southerners took them and threw them out the window.

"Pay the boy, Nicodemus," he said.

Tom scooped up all the old magazines and books he had not been able to sell. He stacked them up in a pile higher than his head. He staggered down the aisle.

Promptly the men threw Tom's load out the window and told Nicodemus to pay. Tom disposed of all his candy and nuts the same way.

A few minutes later he dragged his little trunk down the aisle. He took off his hat, coat, and shoes and laid them on the trunk.

"What have you now?"

"Everything, sir, that I can spare."

The man motioned to the back of the car.

Grinning, Nicodemus dragged the trunk to the door and dumped trunk, clothes and all. Then he dug in the bag and counted out Tom's price—twenty-seven dollars.

Tom paddled happily back to the baggage car in his bare feet. He knew that he must spend the money soon for supplies and new clothes. But he would always keep a warm feeling for the generous Southerners.

During the War between the States, Tom was able to sell extra newspapers. One morning he saw people crowding around the newspaper offices in Detroit. He learned that a big battle had been fought. Many soldiers had been killed and wounded.

Tom went back to the depot. There he asked the telegraph operator to send news of the battle to each station where his train would stop. Then he went to the office of the *Detroit Free Press*. He asked to see the editor.

Two men were in the office where Tom was sent. Quickly he explained that he wanted a thousand papers. He had only enough money to buy three hundred. "I will pay for the rest tomorrow," he promised.

"We'd be crazy to give him a thousand papers on credit," one of the men said. "The boy usually sells only a hundred papers. How do we know he'd pay?"

"Let him have the papers," the other man said.

Crowds were waiting at every station to buy Tom's papers. He saw that a thousand papers would not be enough. So many people were eager to buy that he began to raise the price. First he charged five cents, then ten cents, then fifteen cents. At last he reached Port Huron. A crowd pressed around him.

"The papers are twenty-five cents apiece!

And I haven't enough for everybody," he shouted.

"Here! Here! Let me have one."

Soon Tom sold every paper he had left.

The next morning Tom paid for the extra papers. It seemed to him that he still had an immense amount of money left. He went to a store and bought the batteries he had wanted for so long. He visited Mr. Pullman who promised to make the rack Tom wanted for his laboratory.

"Today I had money to buy what I needed," he said happily. Still, only part of his problem was solved. How could he get the time he needed for his telegraph and for new experiments?

"Papers! Papers!" he cried in the train aisle. While he was selling his papers, he was thinking of a plan. He wished the train would go faster. He could hardly wait to get home.

Mike was waiting at Port Huron with the horse and cart.

"Hurry," said Tom excitedly. He piled the batteries and papers in the cart. "We must stop at Jim's house on the way home."

Tom left all his papers at Jim's house.

"But your pa! He'll be waiting for those papers," said Mike.

Tom grinned. "Can you keep a secret?"

Mike nodded. He liked secrets.

There was a mischievous giggle in Tom's voice. "I forgot my papers at Jim's. *On purpose!*"

Then Tom told Mike his plan. Mike laughed so hard he almost fell off the cart.

"I don't know if it'll work," Mike said. "Your pa likes to read those papers better'n anything."

"Hello, Mother! Hello, Father!" Tom hurried through the sitting room. He saw his father sitting by the lamp. He knew that he was waiting for the papers.

"Your food is ready," called Mrs. Edison.

Tom was halfway down the basement steps. "Got my new batteries. May I hook them up to my telegraph before I eat, please?"

A few minutes later Tom's father went to the basement. "Did you bring the papers, son?" he asked.

"I left them at Jim's." Tom felt a little guilty. He did not look at his father. He was afraid he might give his plan away.

"Say, the batteries are hooked up now. Maybe I could get Jim to send the news over the wire from his house. We know the Morse Code. It would work fine," Tom suggested. He began to tap out a message using the code.

. . . . . — . . . . . "Help!"

. . — . — "O.K." came the reply.

Jim was a little too prompt, thought Tom. He hoped his father would not notice. "Send the news!" he tapped out on the telegraph.

Soon the machine was clicking away. Tom grabbed a pencil and paper. He wrote the news down for his father.

Eleven o'clock, Tom's bedtime, passed. Still the news came in over the wire. Twelve o'clock passed. Then twelve-thirty. At last Tom's father said they must go to bed.

Tom tried his plan for several more nights. Each night he was allowed to stay up until twelve-thirty. He was a little ashamed of the trick he had played. One night he said, "If I could stay up every night—"

"You wouldn't forget to bring home the papers." Tom's father laughed. "I've known what you were up to, young man."

"I only need six hours of sleep," Tom answered. "I can take naps during the day."

"You don't seem to need as much sleep as most boys," Tom's father agreed. "We'll try letting you stay up until twelve-thirty."

Tom was happy. His plan had worked. Now he had the extra time he needed for his experiments.

"Time and money," he said softly. He felt in his pockets. All his money was gone. He remembered that he had spent the last of it for chemicals that day.

CHAPTER EIGHT

· GROWING UP ·

Tom was willing to undertake any job to earn extra money for his laboratory. One night he had a chance to carry a message.

The captain of a big ship had died.

"The ship must leave Detroit in the morning," the owner said. "The ship cannot leave without a captain."

The owner offered to pay Tom fifteen dollars to take a message to a captain who lived fourteen miles from the railroad.

Tom knew the trip would be long and tiresome at night. "I will need to hire another boy to go with me," he said. "I will go if you will pay twenty-five dollars."

"All right. But I expect you to deliver my message without fail," the owner said.

The conductor promised to tell Mike at Port Huron that Tom was working, so that his parents would not worry.

At eight-thirty that evening Tom got off the train at a little station called Ridgeway. The station was dark. Rain was pouring down.

Tom lit two lanterns—one for the boy he had hired and one for himself. Then bravely the two boys set out in the darkness.

Tom would always remember that night. Part of the way was through dense forest. Tall trees looked like strange shapes in lantern light. Rain soaked through Tom's coat and water trickled down his back.

After a while one of the lanterns went out. The flame in the other grew weak. Then it, too, sputtered and died.

The two boys were left in total darkness. They slipped in mud and tripped over logs.

Tom thought of all the stories he had read about wolves and bears.

Once a leaf brushed against his face and frightened him. Once he groped against a moss-covered stump. He thought it was the furry back of a bear. A terrible fear came over him.

"I'm scared! Let's climb a tree and wait till morning," Tom's companion begged.

"Bears can climb trees, too," said Tom, trying to keep his voice steady. "And I promised to deliver the message."

The boys stumbled on. At last a faint light began to appear.

It was morning. Tom's heart sank. Would they be too late with the message?

Ahead a little curl of smoke rose in the sky. How glad Tom was to see the captain's house!

They were in time. The captain drove the boys back to Ridgeway. There they caught the train to Detroit where the ship was waiting.

Tired and bedraggled, Tom curled up on the floor of the baggage car. He thought of the terrible night he had spent.

I should have checked the oil in the lanterns before we started, he decided. Then we would not have been left in darkness. I should have known more about the habits of wild animals. Then I would not have been afraid. I am going to learn more. I am always going to be better prepared for anything I do.

Tom was beginning to think ahead, like a real scientist.

One hot morning in August, 1862, Tom stood on the platform at Mount Clemens station. He could hear the *clickity-click* of the telegraph keys inside. The station agent, Mr. Mackenzie, was receiving a message. Maybe someday I can read a fast telegram like that, Tom thought.

Tom noticed little Jimmy, the agent's two-year-old son, playing on the platform. After a while the boy ran to the tracks. He began to play in the stones between the rails.

Chug! Chug! Chug! A switch engine was moving freight cars. The wheels ground and squeaked.

Chugchugchug! The engine gained speed. A trainman uncoupled the last car.

The car came rolling down the main track. Then it swung to the side track where Jimmy was playing.

Tom dropped his papers and dashed for the boy. He scooped him up in his arms. He felt the rush of wheels and air from the oncoming car. Then everything went black.

The next thing Tom knew, he was being carried into the station. He heard Jimmy crying. He reached up to his burning face and found his hand covered with blood.

"Only scratches," a trainman assured him. "You rushed so fast for the little fellow you both went head-on into the gravel beside the

rails. It was a narrow escape. The car was so close it nicked your heel."

Mackenzie held his son in his arms. The boy had stopped crying, but tears of gratitude streamed down the father's face. "You saved my boy's life," he told Tom.

Tom was embarrassed at being a hero.

"I haven't any money," Mr. Mackenzie went on, "but I want to do something for you.

Didn't you say you'd like to learn telegraphy? I could teach you to be a telegraph operator."

"You could?" Tom grinned happily.

"All aboard!" the conductor shouted.

Tom grabbed his papers. He climbed on the bottom step of the train just as it pulled out.

A few days later Tom had to run for the train. They had stopped near the station at Smith's Creek to take water. Tom got off, hoping to sell extra papers. The train started without him. He had a big stack of papers in his arms. He tried to board the moving train, but his hand slipped.

The conductor reached for Tom, trying to help. Tom's collar slipped from his hands. The train began to pick up speed. The conductor grabbed Tom's ears and pulled him into the car. Tom heard a snapping sound.

Before long he noticed that he could hear only the sounds close to him. He did not mind. He could work at the telegraph keys without hearing other noises. When he was busy in his laboratory no sounds outside bothered him. Even the noise of the train was gone.

Tom was busy and happy. He continued to print his newspaper. And he began to work experiments in college textbooks.

Some days he got off the train at Mount Clemens and studied telegraphy all day. Mr. Mackenzie was a good teacher, and Tom learned fast. He found that telegraphers had a language all their own. The number *seventy-three* meant good wishes. *Twenty-three* meant an accident or bad luck.

Tom loved his traveling laboratory. But it was not easy to work on a moving train. The baggage car swayed and rocked and jolted.

One day, while Tom was working, the train gave a terrible jerk. Papers flew across the car. Chemicals bounced off the table.

In his rack Tom had a stick of phosphorous —a chemical used in making matches. The phosphorous fell and skidded across the floor. It acted like hundreds of matches all scratched at once.

Suddenly the inside of the car was in flames. Tom's papers caught fire. Even the wooden floor of the car began to burn.

Tom was frightened. "Fire! Fire!" he cried. He whipped at the flames with his coat.

The conductor heard Tom's cries and came running. He grabbed a bucket of sand from the next car. He pulled off his own coat to smother the flames. At last he put out the fire. But the car was damaged inside.

"I've stood all this foolishness I'm going to," the conductor stormed. "From now on the trainboy sticks to papers and candy."

Angrily he ripped Tom's precious rack of chemicals from the wall. At the next stop he ordered Tom off the train. He threw everything Tom owned out the baggage-car door.

Sadly Tom watched the train puff away.

Then he stooped to pick up what was left of his laboratory.

The next day Tom got off the train at Mount Clemens to take his telegraphy lesson. He was still sad over the loss of his traveling laboratory.

"Well, you weren't aiming to be a trainboy all your life, were you?" Mr. Mackenzie put his arm around Tom's shoulders. "You saved my son's life. Now I'm going to make you the best operator on the whole line. I'll teach you everything I know. Then I'll get you a job on the railroad."

"A railroad telegraph operator?" Tom had heard the job paid well. It would give him time for experiments.

Suddenly he felt happy again. "You're always talking about me rescuing your son, Mr. Mackenzie," he said. "Now I wonder if you aren't the one who has rescued *me*."

CHAPTER NINE

• "LIGHTNING SLINGING" •

"Two things I can't figure out." Tom brushed back a lock of hair from his eyes.

"Shoot! But let me have the questions one at a time, please." Mr. Mackenzie was used to Tom's questions.

"Well, first I can't figure out why people call telegraph operators *lightning slingers*."

Mr. Mackenzie laughed. "Just wait, boy, till you're sending a message and lightning hits the wire. Why, I've seen fellows get electric shocks that knocked them clear across the room."

Tom's eyes were big. "Why don't they stop sending in storms?" he asked.

"It's during storms a message might be needed most. What if a bridge is washed out? Word must get through to stop the train. Any minute an important message might come over the wire. It might prevent a wreck. It might save many lives.

"We'll stick at the keys—and even fight lightning—to get a message through. That's why we're called lightning slingers."

Tom was thoughtful for a moment. Then eagerly he asked the next question.

"Mr. Mackenzie, how does electricity carry the dots and dashes over the wire?"

Mr. Mackenzie pushed his fingers through his red hair. "I don't know that, my boy. Nobody knows. I wonder if anyone ever will know."

Click, click. The key began to tap out a message.

"Take it down, Tom. It's from Detroit."

Tom reached for a pencil and paper. Already his mind was changing the dots, dashes, and spaces into words. "Stop Train No. 14. Hold package left on first coach."

Mr. Mackenzie was pleased. "You write clear and neat—and fast. That will be a big advantage in taking messages. Tom, my boy, you soak up learning like a sponge. Before long you will know everything I can teach you. After that all you will need is practice."

Tom studied with Mr. Mackenzie almost four months. Later Mr. Mackenzie helped him get a job. Tom was sixteen years old when he went to Stratford Junction, Canada, as night telegraph operator.

Night work suited him perfectly. During the day he had time to experiment. He had ideas for improving telegraph equipment. Always he was searching for the answer to his question: How does electricity carry messages along the wire?

One day an old Scottish line repairman

gave him an answer he never forgot. "Just imagine you had a dachshund dog. Believe that the dog was long enough for its tail to be in Edinburgh while its head was in London. If you pulled its tail in Edinburgh it would bark in London."

"I can understand that," Tom laughed. Then he grew serious. "But it's what goes on *inside* the dog that bothers me. What really goes through the wire? Will I ever find out?"

Few messages came over the wire at night. Often Tom fell asleep. Every hour he must open the key and send the message: *Six*. This message showed that he was awake and on the job.

The night watchman at the station woke Tom every hour so that he could report.

One night Tom had an idea. He would make a small notched wheel and attach it to the station clock. He would wire the device to his sending key. He believed his *Six* message could be sent while he slept. He would not have to bother the watchman again.

Tom's invention worked perfectly. Every hour the key opened and clicked out six dots.

Every night Tom reported—every hour, on the hour. His message was so regular that the train dispatcher was amazed. But when he signaled back, he often had no reply.

One night the dispatcher tried again and again to reach Tom. Finally he sent an assistant to Stratford to see what was wrong.

Tom was sleeping at the desk. Just then the hands of the clock showed it was midnight. There was a strange spinning sound. The key tapped out six dots.

The assistant looked in wonder at the device Tom had made. Then he shook Tom awake.

After that, Tom tried to pay more attention to his work. But before long he was discharged for neglecting his duties.

Then, for five years Tom wandered from city to city, working as a telegraph operator. Sometimes he held a job for only a few weeks or months. Often he went hungry. But always he found time to read and to experiment.

In 1864, he took a job with the Western Union Telegraph Company in Indianapolis, Indiana.

Tom soon found that he could not write down news stories fast enough. News often came over the wire at the rate of forty words a minute. He realized that he must gain more speed in writing.

Meanwhile he brought two old machines to the office. They were called Morse Registers. He adjusted one machine so that it recorded dots and dashes on paper. In this way the machine recorded the messages as they came over the wire.

Tom made the other machine into a repeater. It repeated the dots and dashes from the paper. The repeater could be set as fast or as slow as he wished. It gave him time to write out a perfect copy of the messages.

One day, when news was coming in fast, Tom was caught using his machines. The manager ordered Tom to take them away.

That night Tom carried his heavy machines back through dark streets to his room.

"My machines work," he said softly. "I will keep them until I have a laboratory of my own. Then I will make them work even better."

Tom quickened his steps. An idea was growing in his mind. Perhaps I can make the repeater print out words instead of just dots and dashes, he thought. Someday I will make an automatic telegraph.

Before long Tom moved to Cincinnati, Ohio. He worked hard to increase his speed in taking messages, and he was promoted to first-class operator. At last he could write fast enough to take any message off the wire.

The old telegraph office where Tom worked in Cincinnati was overrun with rats. Any time of day or night a rat might run out of a hole and devour an operator's lunch. The rats were afraid of no one. They were a terrible pest.

"I'll fix them," Tom promised. "I'll make a rat paralyzer."

"I'd like to see you. We've tried everything, including poison," said Milt Adams, who had become Tom's good friend.

The other operators watched while Tom set to work. He placed two flat pieces of metal on the floor. Then he attached the metal pieces to a battery.

Soon a rat jumped out from a hole in the wall and began to run across the floor. Its front feet touched one piece of metal while its hind feet touched the other.

Pfft! The rat fell over dead—electrocuted.

People in Cincinnati heard of Edison's rat

paralyzer. They flocked to see the invention.

Before long the manager of the office decided the curious people disturbed business more than the rats. He ordered Tom to dispose of his invention.

A few weeks later Adams moved north. Tom went south to Louisville, Kentucky. There he found the telegraph equipment old and rotting. Lightning seemed especially bad.

"Lightning strikes the wires making an explosion like a cannon shot. This is no place for a man with a weak heart," he wrote Mr. Mackenzie. Now he knew the real meaning of *lightning slinging*.

CHAPTER TEN

· IN BOSTON ·

The old office in Louisville was a good place for Tom to try out his ideas. He thought of many ways to improve the equipment. Then the company moved to new offices. The manager called in the operators to warn them.

"Our new equipment is now in its proper place. You are to make no changes. Batteries are to be used only for your regular work."

Tom paid little attention to the warning. One night, while he was experimenting, he spilled some acid. It ran through the floor into the manager's room below. It ruined the manager's desk and his new carpet.

The manager was very angry. "We want

operators, not experimenters," he told Tom. "You may take your pay and get out."

Tom had spent almost two years in Louisville. His parents were growing old, and his mother was ill. He knew they were lonely. He decided to go home for a visit.

After a few weeks in Port Huron, Tom wrote Milt Adams asking about opportunities in Boston.

"Come on. I have a job for you in Western Union's main office," Milt replied.

Tom arrived in Boston on a cold winter day in 1868. He wore a long linen coat called a duster. His jeans were tucked into high boots that were too big. His hat had a hole in the brim.

"Can this strange-looking fellow be the operator Adams sent for?" the men in the office asked. They wondered if he knew much about telegraphy. They whispered a plan to try him out.

The operators grinned when Tom reported for work that evening. They had wired the New York office, "A greenhorn from the West is taking the news tonight. Put your fastest sender on that end."

Tom sat down at his desk. He did not know that the man at the other end of the wire was the fastest operator in the East.

Faster and faster the news came in. Faster and faster Tom wrote. He looked up and saw the men watching. Suddenly he knew they were playing a trick on him.

His pen raced across the paper. But he kept up with the sender. Then the New York man began to make mistakes in spelling. He let the key stick so the words would not be clear.

Tom had much experience taking reports under all sorts of conditions. He was not fooled or bothered. He could tell the right words almost before they came over the wire.

At last he thought it was time to end the

joke. He opened the key and tapped out a message.

"Say, why don't you change off and send with your other foot?"

The men in the office roared with laughter. They knew the joke was on them. They shook hands with Tom. "Might have known a friend of Milt's would be O.K.," they said.

Tom walked to the cheap rooming house where he was to stay with Milt. The wind off the Atlantic Ocean was raw. His duster gave little protection. But he was not thinking of the cold. He was not thinking of his success as a telegraph operator or of the friends he had just made.

That afternoon he had been in some of the stores in Boston. He had seen exciting machines and devices. He had seen electric clocks, new telegraph equipment, and stock tickers. These devices filled his mind. He could hardly wait to get back to his experiments.

In the daytime Tom experimented in the little shop of a friend who made electric clocks and telegraph equipment. Tom's space in the shop was no bigger than a good-sized closet.

Often he was still thinking of his experiments after he went to work at night. He loved to use his ideas over and over in different ways. One night he was working again on an idea he had used several years before.

Someone in the Western Union office shouted, "Here comes the cake man."

Tom grinned. He looked at the clock. It was midnight—time for the cake man to bring their lunch.

The cockroaches in the building came running. They seemed to know when the cake man was coming.

The operators crowded around Tom's desk. "Turn on your magic cockroach exterminator. We want to see how it works," they urged.

On the wall over his desk Tom had pasted

two strips of tinfoil so that they could be attached to a battery. Now he connected the wires.

The roaches swarmed up and down the wall. They were after the food the men had bought.

Pfft! Pfft! Sparks crackled.

The moment a roach's legs touched both strips of tinfoil at once an electric circuit was completed. Electricity ran through the roach's body and it was killed instantly. Tom's roach exterminator was as successful as his rat paralyzer had been. Dead cockroaches piled up on the floor back of his desk.

Not long after Tom made his exterminator, he accidentally tried the same experiment on himself. He touched, at one time, both poles of a coil attached to a battery. Thus he completed an electric circuit with his own body, much as the rats and cockroaches had done with theirs.

Tom felt the electric current surge through his body in a terrible shock. The current was not strong enough to paralyze him. But it made his hands stick to the coil.

He pulled and pulled, trying to free himself. The battery was on the shelf above the sink where he was working. At last he shut his eyes, and gave a tremendous jerk.

Down the battery crashed! The electric circuit was broken. Tom could free his hands.

But the battery splashed acid over Tom's face when it fell. The acid burned like fire.

Quickly he washed the burns with water, which helped to stop the pain.

Tom looked in the mirror. Dark yellow marks covered his face where the acid had struck him. Then Tom looked down at the new suit he had bought to please Milt.

"Oh," he groaned as he saw the big holes the acid had made. New skin would grow on his face in time, he reasoned, but he knew the suit was ruined. "It serves me right for paying thirty dollars for it!" he said.

Tom's experience with the power of electricity only made him more eager than ever to experiment further. He found books written by a British scientist, Michael Faraday. Faraday explained how he had made electricity go through a coil of wire. Tom tried the experiment. By moving a magnet up and down in a coil, he also could make electric current.

I have no time for sleep, thought Tom. But he wanted to see Milt. He found him at their rooming house, and the two rushed out for breakfast. Excitedly Tom told Milt about his experiment with the magnet. "At last," he said, "I am beginning to understand more about what goes on *inside* an electric wire."

Milt watched Tom eating baked beans and brown bread. He saw Tom's burned face and his ruined suit. He shook his head.

"Tom, old man," he said affectionately, "you don't give a hang what you eat or what you wear. Nevertheless, I think you're going to be a great inventor someday—if you live."

A smile flashed across Tom's face. He looked admiringly at his well-dressed friend. But his reply was thoughtful. "Milt, I have got so much to do, and life is so short. I am going to hustle."

CHAPTER ELEVEN

FROM IDEAS TO INVENTIONS

Ideas and more ideas filled Tom's mind. Hustle as he would, he soon saw that he could not work on as many of them as he wished.

"I should work on one idea. Patent it. Then sell it," he said. "Perhaps I could make enough money to get a laboratory.

"A laboratory—" Tom repeated the last words wistfully. His idea of success had not changed since he was a boy. But now he knew that it would take a great deal of money for the equipment he wanted.

In the fall of 1868, he decided to invent a vote recorder. He had learned, in the telegraph office, how long it took to record votes in Congress. Sometimes news stories were delayed many hours while Congress voted.

"I will invent a machine that can record all the votes in less than a minute," Tom said. "I will sell it to the government."

Day after day Tom worked on his invention in the little shop of his friend. At night he worked in the telegraph office. Tom had little time for sleep. But even a little rest made him feel refreshed and ready to go on.

Tom spent all his money on the vote recorder. Soon he applied for a patent. This would protect his invention from being copied. But he needed more money to complete the machine and take it to Washington.

"I'll loan you a hundred dollars and go with you," an operator named Roberts offered.

How excited Tom was when he and Roberts boarded the train for Washington! They carried Tom's first patented invention.

Tom and his friend demonstrated his invention before a committee of Congress. The machine worked perfectly.

By pressing one button on his desk a congressman could vote "Yes." By pressing another button he could vote "No." The machine showed clearly how each man voted. In less than a minute all voting was recorded.

The chairman of the committee shook his head. "Your invention works well. It works too well. We do not want it here." He made Tom understand that congressmen often delayed voting on purpose. Sometimes they did not want people to know how they voted.

Riding the train back to Boston, Roberts noticed that Tom was quiet.

"You must be very discouraged," he said.

"Oh," answered Tom, aroused from other thoughts. "I have so many ideas I want to see work. But from now on, I will be sure an invention is wanted before I work on it."

Again Tom was lost in thought. He looked

out the train window. A telegraph wire on poles followed beside the tracks.

A message is going through that wire now, Tom said to himself. There are other messages waiting to go through.

This was not the first time he had thought of the crowded telegraph wires. Every night, while he sat at the keys, messages came rushing, rushing. Some messages came over the wire late. Sometimes the operators fought for the wire. People complained to the telegraph companies because they did not have enough wires.

Suddenly he knew the idea he must work on next. A multiple telegraph! That was it. He would control the current. Two messages, perhaps even more, could be sent over the same wire at one time!

Tom was planning his next invention!

CHAPTER TWELVE

• POCKETS FULL OF MONEY •

Tom resigned from his job as a Boston telegraph operator in 1869. By this time his invention for carrying two messages over one wire at one time was ready to test.

He completed the work in his friend's little shop in Boston. When he needed to experiment with long wires he strung them on the tops of buildings, or used the wires already there.

"I am a telegraph man," Tom would say when he wanted to climb to a roof.

"Yes, yes. Go right up," the owners always said. They had no idea what Tom was really doing on their roof tops.

Tom called his invention Edison's Double Transmitter. The Atlantic and Pacific Telegraph Company promised to buy it if it worked. Tom had to borrow money to complete his work. The company test of Tom's invention was made on the wire between Rochester and New York.

Tom traveled hopefully to Rochester. But the man placed at the New York end of the wire did not understand the equipment. Tom stayed in Rochester a week trying to get his double transmitter to work. Finally he realized that men who tried to operate his invention must have special training in how to use it. The test was a failure.

When Tom returned to Boston with his invention he found it worked perfectly. He decided to go back to New York and try to interest another company in his double transmitter.

Tom spent all his money for a ticket and

arrived in New York with empty pockets. He found two old friends he had known as a telegrapher. One loaned him a dollar for food. The other friend was working for the Gold Indicator Company.

"You can sleep here on the floor of the battery room until you get work," this friend suggested.

So Tom slept on the floor at night. For a while he forgot the invention he had come to New York to sell. He wanted to study the exciting machines which the company owned. He was especially interested in the master machine that controlled other machines, called stock tickers. They worked somewhat like an automatic telegraph system.

Tick, tick, tick. It was Tom's third day in New York but he still was watching the fascinating master machine. It was ticking off numbers which showed the price of gold.

Three hundred tickers which the machine

controlled were ticking off the same numbers in different offices all over the city. Tom thrilled at the thought. He had already done some work on a ticker of his own. But this was his first chance to watch a big ticker system working.

Suddenly, as Tom watched, there was a terrible grinding noise. The machine stopped.

All the tickers the machine controlled stopped also. Messenger boys from three hundred offices began to stream in. "Our ticker is broken!" they cried.

Excited workmen looked at the machine that controlled all the stock tickers. They did not know what was the matter.

The president rushed from his office. "Can't somebody fix it?" he asked.

Tom stepped up. "I believe I know what the trouble is, sir," he said.

"Then fix it," the president ordered.

Tom found that a spring had broken and

fallen into the gears. In two hours he had the machine working again.

The president was so pleased that he placed Tom in charge of all the machines. He paid him three hundred dollars a month.

Tom was happy. He liked the work. In his spare time he could continue his inventions. He would try to make his multiple telegraph carry more than two messages at one time. "And now I will invent a stock ticker that will not break so easily," he declared.

General Marshall Lefferts, president of the Gold and Stock Telegraph Company, asked Tom to improve his stock-ticker machines. Tom made new machines that worked much better than the old ones.

General Lefferts was pleased with Tom's inventions. "How much do you want for them?" he asked.

Tom hesitated. He hoped to get five thousand dollars, but he would be satisfied with three thousand. "How much do you think they are worth?" he finally asked.

"Forty thousand dollars."

For a moment Tom thought he could not have heard correctly. Then he said, "That sounds fair."

He would not allow himself to believe his good fortune until he received the check. Then happily he rushed to the bank. But he had never before cashed a check. When the check was passed back to him to sign, Tom thought it was no good. In dismay he returned to General Lefferts' office.

The general had a good laugh. Then he sent his secretary back to the bank with Tom. The teller grinned. He counted out small bills —stacks of them. "There you are, young man," he said. "Forty thousand dollars!"

Tom did not know what to do with so much money. He loaded all his pockets. Then he stuffed his shirt.

"Who would have thought I'd ever be *bulging* with money?" he laughed. But, going home, he was uncomfortable. He was sure every robber in New York must be waiting for him. He sat up all night guarding his money.

The next morning he went back to Lefferts' office. The general's secretary helped him open an account at the bank.

"Whew!" Tom sighed in relief. He was glad to have the money safe.

Now he could make big plans for spending it. He would rent a shop and laboratory. He would buy the equipment he wanted. And he would hire men to work on his ideas.

Tom smiled. At the age of twenty-three his dreams were fast coming true. He found a pen and a piece of paper. In clear, straight letters he began to write happily:

Dear Mother and Father—

CHAPTER THIRTEEN

• THE TALKING MACHINE •

Inventions and more inventions poured from Edison's laboratory. Workers in the patent office in Washington marveled that a man could invent so many new things.

Tom had to hire more and more help to carry on his work. He had rented a shop in Newark, New Jersey. In 1876 the shop was too crowded, and he decided to build a big new plant in Menlo Park. By this time Tom Edison was married. When he and his wife had a little girl, he called her Dot. And when a baby boy came, his proud father called him Dash. Tom Edison bought a big home for his family near his new laboratory.

There was no invention too big or too small for him. He was willing to work on anything he thought was needed.

His wife sent sandwiches to the plant for his lunches. Sometimes she wrapped them in a damp cloth. She put paper on the outside to keep them fresh.

Often she worried. "Were the sandwiches too dry? Were they too moist?"

"I do not care what I have to eat," Tom told her, smiling. "But to please you I will invent something to wrap sandwiches in and keep them fresh." So he invented waxed paper.

As soon as Tom Edison finished an invention he set to work perfecting it. Usually other inventions followed.

He had improved his early inventions to record telegraph messages and repeat the dots and dashes. And he had even invented the automatic machine which printed messages in words as they came off the wire.

Somehow, Edison had found time to work on his multiple telegraph. And he had successfully invented and sold quadruplex telegraphy. This invention made it possible to send four messages—two each way—over one wire at one time.

Edison had also worked on Alexander Graham Bell's telephone. He had made a separate receiver and mouthpiece for it. And his ideas were the basis for successful microphones.

One evening in his new laboratory Edison began to think about the possibility of reproducing real sounds.

From a drawer he pulled out a little toy. He had made it while he was working on the telephone. The toy showed how a thin piece of metal, called a diaphragm, could take up sound waves, or vibrations. Tom Edison shouted into a small tube, or mouthpiece, of the toy. A little paper man attached to the diaphragm moved back and forth.

"Mr. Edison, what are you making?" John Kruesi had heard the shouts as he passed Edison's door. Kruesi was a skilled assistant who had been educated in Switzerland.

"I am inventing a machine that will make a record of talking. And it will talk back."

Kruesi shook his head. "I have seen you make many wonderful things, Mr. Edison. But that is impossible."

Quickly Edison began to make a sketch of a cylinder with grooves around the surface. The cylinder could be turned with a handle. Over the cylinder he would place tinfoil. The soft metal would record the movements of the diaphragm easily, he reasoned.

A point attached to the diaphragm would move, much as the paper man in his toy moved. The point could make marks on the tinfoil. When the diaphragm was run back over the marks on the tinfoil, it should repeat the sounds.

Tom Edison finished his drawing and gave it to Kruesi.

Some hours later Kruesi finished the machine he made from the drawing. He brought it to Edison's office. A group of interested workers followed. "I'll bet a box of cigars it doesn't work," said one.

Carefully Edison placed a piece of tinfoil around the cylinder. Then he began to speak into the mouthpiece. He turned the handle as he spoke.

He said the first words that came to his mind. Then he set the diaphragm back to the beginning of the cylinder.

For a moment he held his breath. He dared to hope only for a few faint sounds. If he could get sounds—sounds anything like a human voice—he might be started on a new invention.

Edison began to turn the handle. Then clearly his own voice came out into the room:

"Mary had a little lamb
Its fleece was white as snow,
And everywhere that Mary went
The lamb was sure to go."

The men stood with their mouths open.
Mein Himmel!" Kruesi broke the silence.
"It talks! It talks!" the men shouted.

No one was more surprised than Edison himself. On his first attempt he had invented a talking machine.

"I will call it a phonograph," he said.

The men stayed up all night. They recited and they sang. Everybody had to try out the new machine.

News of the wonderful invention spread over the world. Edison was asked to show his machine in Washington, where he was invited to the White House.

"Magic!" people cried when they heard the phonograph the first time.

Edison smiled shyly in a way people loved. He tried to explain, "It is really a very simple machine."

CHAPTER FOURTEEN

• THE MAGIC LIGHT •

Edison knew that he would work for months on his phonograph to make it perfect. For a while he left his phonograph and other inventions in sound to turn to light.

Many people used gas for lighting. Others still used old-fashioned oil lamps, or even wax candles. Edison believed he could furnish cheaper and better light with electricity.

In September, 1878, he visited the shop of William Wallace in Ansonia, Connecticut. Mr. Wallace made an electric light called the arc light. This light burned in the open air. It gave off an unpleasant odor. New parts had to be used every few hours. It was expensive.

Edison believed that Mr. Wallace had done a great deal of good work. He bought one of the arc lights to take back to Menlo Park.

"I am convinced that electricity should be used for lighting," he said, shaking Mr. Wallace's hand. Then his eyes twinkled. "But I believe I can beat you at making electric lights."

So Edison began the most exciting experiments he had ever done. He was determined to make an electric light that would glow with heat. He would call it the incandescent lamp. "I must make it cheaply enough for everybody to use," he said.

Thomas Edison had started one of the greatest inventions of all time.

Day and night he worked on the new light. He hardly took time to eat. Sometimes he slept for a few minutes in his office. But even as he slept his mind seemed to be working. He had new ideas to try as soon as he awoke.

Edison hired a glass blower to make bulbs. He bought pumps to pump air out of the bulbs. And he thought of new ways to control electric current. He tried many materials to burn inside the bulbs. Sometimes he wondered if anything in the whole world could stand the intense heat necessary to furnish light.

For more than a year Edison worked on his light. Then one day he called in Charles Batchelor, one of his best scientists.

"Bring in the others who have worked on the light," he said.

"Have you got it at last, boss?" Batchelor asked.

"No," answered Edison, "but I want the men to see this bulb."

Soon John Kruesi, Ludwig Boehm, Francis Jehl, Martin Force, Francis Upton, and William Hammer rushed into Edison's office. For some weeks the men had been excited. Edison had spent thousands of dollars. Was he ready to announce an invention? The eyes of the men were bright and questioning.

Edison knew that people wondered how he obtained such devotion and loyalty from the men who worked for him. Sometimes they worked all night without a thought of going home. Edison believed his men were as interested as he was in the inventions at the Menlo Park laboratory.

Now "the boss" smiled as he shook his head. "This bulb is not the answer. We have gone as far as we can in this direction. I want you to see the result."

The men crowded around as Edison turned on a switch and a bulb lighted. It gave off a bright, white light.

"What's wrong with *this?*" asked Jehl.

"This light is not practical," answered Edison. "In the first place, it would cost too much. It took thirty feet of fine platinum wire rolled on a spool."

"Thirty feet!" Jehl exclaimed. He knew that platinum was more expensive than gold.

"Now watch while I turn the electricity a little stronger."

Pfft! Before their eyes, the light burned out. In less than a second the bulb had turned black. The stronger current had melted the platinum inside.

Edison went on to explain that in using platinum he had made an important discovery. "When the electricity is turned on, still more air can be pumped from the bulbs. While a bulb burns, we will pump it again. Then we will seal it tightly."

By pumping a bulb a second time, Edison had discovered a way to get rid of the gas which the first heating of the light caused.

Edison wanted his men to understand what he was doing. They had spent months working on experiments they might have thought useless. Perhaps they would have to spend months more before he made a satisfactory light.

The men started to leave. Each felt new hope and confidence and pride. Each showed a new excitement.

"Wait, Batchelor," Edison said.

Just then an office boy rushed in. "Mrs. Edison said she couldn't imagine what you wanted with ordinary cotton sewing thread," he said. "But she gave it to me. Are you going to use thread in your new light?"

"Perhaps," smiled the inventor, reaching for the thread.

Quickly he cut off several small pieces. He bent each piece into a tiny loop shaped like a horseshoe.

"Carbonize these pieces of thread," Edison said to Batchelor. To carbonize them, the threads were baked in a hot oven until they were burned black.

"But I thought you had given up carbon

for light." Batchelor was plainly surprised.

"I am going back to carbon," said Edison. "We can now pump more air from the bulbs. Carbon is still the best material I have found.

"Bring the thread to me as soon as it is done. I will be waiting. And have more bulbs made," Edison added.

Several hours later Batchelor brought the threads. They were burned black and hard. Quickly Edison attached one in a glass bulb.

When the air was pumped out, the bulb was sealed. It was ready for the test. Edison turned on the electricity.

The bulb burned for ten, twelve, fifteen minutes—longer than a carbon bulb had burned before. Still it burned.

Night came. The bulb was burning. The men began to collect in Edison's office. They did not want to go home.

All night long the bulb burned. Morning came. The bulb was still burning.

Edison rubbed his tired eyes.

Lights. Lights. Everywhere he looked, he could see nothing but lights. He knew that he had watched the light too long. At last he lay down on the desk. "Wake me up the minute the light goes out," he said.

When Edison awoke, the light was still burning. It burned for forty hours. Even while it burned, the inventor was thinking of ways to improve it.

"Carbonized paper should work better than thread," he reasoned. He rolled paper into a thin little roll as fine as thread and sent it to be baked into carbon.

He was right. The paper carbon burned indefinitely!

People began to read and hear the news of the wonderful light. "Edison is a wizard," they declared. "Now he has invented a magic light."

CHAPTER FIFTEEN

A WIZARD LIGHTS THE WORLD

Thomas Alva Edison invented his first successful electric light on October 21, 1879. For several weeks after that, the men in his laboratory in Menlo Park worked day and night. New tools and machinery must be invented to manufacture the new lights. By December 21, many of the lights were in use in the laboratory.

Edison did not want people to think his light was magic. He planned to have an exhibit so everyone who wished might see it. He decided to invite the public to Menlo Park on New Year's Eve.

Everybody in the laboratory worked frantically during the next days. Hundreds of lights were made. Lights were placed throughout the laboratory and in Edison's home and even along the streets.

Three thousand people came from far and near to see the wizard's light on New Year's Eve. Horses and buggies and wagons filled the streets at Menlo Park. And special trains came from New York, bringing many important people. When the trains pulled in, bells were ringing. Everything was dark. Then a switch was pushed. Suddenly hundreds of lights went on at once.

Edison looked up at a window of his home. There, with his family, he had watched the lights tested earlier in the evening. He smiled as he remembered his son's wide eyes. Dot's arms had held him tightly.

"Oh," she had cried, "it's a beautiful fairyland. Did you make all those lights, Daddy?"

"Mr. Edison, did you hear us?" An official

of New York was shouting in his ear. "How long would it take you to light New York?"

"New York?" His lights shining out from the windows of tall buildings in a city! His lights making the city streets a great white way! For a moment he was a little breathless. Then his voice came clearly. "Give me two years, and you could have a good showing."

"Happy New Year! Happy New Year!" the gay crowd cried. The train bell rang. Soon all the visitors were gone.

Slowly Edison walked back to his laboratory. He picked up a pencil and began to draw. It would take a huge power plant to furnish electricity for a big city.

His thoughts were racing. "If electric power can be furnished for light, it can be used for other purposes," he said. "Motors of all sorts can be made to do all kinds of work. Electric engines can be made for trains!"

Thomas Edison was thirty-two years old

on this eve of his exciting invention in light. Already he had given the world some of the most wonderful inventions ever known. Yet he knew that his work was just beginning.

Hundreds of inventions in light and sound and motion pictures were waiting for him to find their secrets. Men and women and boys and girls all over the world were waiting for each new idea.

In one end of his laboratory Edison kept an organ on which he could pick out tunes. He sat down at the organ.

The notes from the organ began softly. And softly Edison spoke. "I must work, work. I must do everything I can for the happiness of man while I am in this world."

The music swelled, filling his beloved laboratory. Inside and outside his new lights were burning. They had turned darkness into light.